Wolves belong to the animal family of 'canids'; they are related to jackals, red foxes and African wild dogs and are a close relative of domestic dogs. In fact, a husky looks just like a small wolf, and you could almost mistake a German Shepherd for a wolf.

The wolf is strong and powerful. Its long legs are good for chasing prey over long distances and its large foot grips well on rocks and ice. It has a thick fur coat to help trap body heat, and a bushy tail. In snowy lands, wolves' fur turns white so they can hide and get close to their prey.

Wolves work together to pull down prey like elk, moose, bison and wild boar. At full speed a wolf could reach 35 miles per hour but only briefly. Their 42 sharp teeth and powerful jaws are good for grabbing and for crushing. Have you ever been told not to 'wolf down' your food?

Wolves live in the woods and forests of Europe, Asia and North America, as well as in plains, tundra and deserts. From being nearly extinct in Europe in the 1960s, they have made a comeback.

The pack is the key to wolves' success and each member has its status in the group. The leader carries its tail higher – hence the phrase 'to be top dog' – while a submissive wolf crouches, turns its ears down and whines.

Wolves have a litter of one to ten pups. The pups weigh 400 grams at birth but by late autumn have grown to about 35 kilos. At first the pups stay in the den suckling but after a month they leave and then get scraps of food from the adults in the pack.

Wolves may bark, with a 'woof', should there be a threat close by. But the famous sound, which you hear in films and read about in books, is howling. They don't in fact howl at the moon but do so to put off other wolves from coming into their territory. There are many tales, like 'Little Red Riding Hood', about scary wolves, but in real life wolves would rather keep away from humans.

Interesting fact: There are many reports of lost children living with wolves. One sad but true case was of two girls in India who were raised by wolves, as in 'The Jungle Book'. Some villagers mistook them for wolf cubs at first, because they ran on their hands and knees and ate red meat.